2/17

BEYOND RUBIK'S CUBE

HOW TO INVENT

Lynn Huggins-Cooper

QEB

QEB Publishing

Created for QEB Publishing, Inc. by Tall Tree Ltd
Editors: Emma Marriott and Jon Richards
Designers: Jonathan Vipond and Malcolm Parchment
Illustrator: Tanja Komadina
Cover Photography: Michael Wicks

QEB Project Editor: Tasha Percy
QEB Editorial Director: Victoria Garrard
QEB Art Director: Laura Roberts-Jensen

Copyright © QEB Publishing, Inc. 2014

Published in the United States in 2014 by
QEB Publishing, Inc.
3 Wrigley, Suite A
Irvine, CA 92618

www.qed-publishing.co.uk

A CIP record for this book is available from the Library of Congress.

ISBN 978 1 60992 629 8

Printed in China

Website information is correct at the time of going to press. However, the publisher cannot accept liability for any information or links found on third-party websites.

WORDS IN **BOLD** ARE FOUND IN THE GLOSSARY

Picture credits

(t=top, b=bottom, l=left, r=right, c=centre, fc=front cover, bc=back cover)

04-05: c Sergiy Zavgorodny, cr Gloria Nicol/Getty Images, tr, Bruce Bi, bl Nation Media, 08-09: tl Time Life Pictures/Getty Images, (cl Acdx, ctr Tomruen at en.wikipedia, tr Pag2006, cbr Oldsoft, br Techno Source) bl, bcl, bcr Denis Finnin, cbl © Heritage Image Partnership Ltd/Alamy, br Ed Simkins, 10-11: l Getty Images, ctr Maximilian Stock Ltd, cr Acdx, br AFP/Getty Images, 12-13: cl © AlamyCelebrity/Alamy, tr Getty Images, 14-15: cl © Bettmann/Corbis, cr GNU Free Documentation license/ Nissen Trampoline Company, 16-17: l © Library of Congress - digital ve/Science Faction/Corbis, cl SSPL/Science Museum, bl public domain, cr SSPL via Getty Images, tr © Hulton-Deutsch Collection/Corbis, bcr Fletcher6 Creative Commons Attribution-Share Alike 3.0 Unported license, br © Bettmann/Corbis, 18-19: c Arvind Balaraman, br Monkey Business Images, 20-21: bl Time Life Pictures/Getty Images, c © Voisin/phanie/Phanie Sarl/Corbis, br © Amelie-Benoist/BSIP/Corbis, 22-23: cl SSPL via Getty Images, bl Getty Images, bc tetedelacourse Creative Commons Attribution-Share Alike 2.0 Generic license, br SSPL/Science Museum, cr Getty Images, tr SSPL via Getty Images, cr Herbert Kratky, bcr Science Photo Library, br ollyy, 24-25: c Maksim Shmeljov, tr National Geographic/Getty Images, 26-27: c AP/Press Association/Larry McCormack, tr Jordan Tan, 28-29: tc Denis Finnin, bc doomu, cr SSPL/Science Museum, 30-31: bl © Bettmann/Corbis, cr The Advertising Archives, br Erik C Pendzich/Rex Features, 32-33: l © Imaginechina/Corbis, r courtesy Siemens AG, Munich/Berlin, tr courtesy Xbox Kinect, bl Chris Rand Creative Commons Attribution-Share Alike 3.0 Unported license, bcl, bc, bcr Evan-Amos public domain, c Siemens, br Barone Firenze, 34-35: l 3drenderings, cr Getty Images, tr Getty Images, 36-37: bl Ross Parry Agency, tr © Michael Runkel/Robert Harding World Imagery/Corbis, br Emmeline Watkins/Science Photo Library, 38-39: l Brady-Handy Photograph Collection, public domain, t Christliches Medienmagazin, bl Winai Tepsuttinun, bcl Dmitrij Skorobogatov, bc djem/Shutterstock, bcr Apple, br Apple, c Bevan Goldswain, tr Apple, , 40-41: l © Caro / Alamy, r © Cesar Okada/iStock, 42-43: l Private Collection/Bridgeman Art Library, 44-45: cl Yojik, t Aljawad Creative Commons Attribution 3.0 Unported license, bl Joseph Nicéphore Niépce, public domain, bcl SSPL via Getty Images, tcr Morio, Creative Commons Attribution-Share Alike 3.0 Unported license, r Jaros, bcr SSPL via Getty Images, br Andy.H.Cheng, Creative Commons Attribution 3.0 Unported license, 46-47: tr cr Denis Finnin, c © Matthieu Paley/Corbis, tr © K.J. Historical/Corbis, 48-49: bl PM Images, r courtesy St. Andrew's Café School for Boys', 50-51: cl XXLPhoto, bl Ed Simkins, r Christopher Furlong/ Getty Images, tc ndoeljindoel, r Sergio Stakhnyk, 52-53: l © Jochen Tack/imagebroker/Corbis, c Chris Ayers Photography/SSP, 54-55: ct Danita Delimont, bl Getty Images, bc akg-images, cr Valentyn Volkov, tcr © Mary Evans Picture Library/Alamy cr © Antiques & Collectables/Alamy, br piotreknik, cl Valentyn Volkov/Shutterstock, 56-57: l public domain, tr © Illustrated London News Ltd/Mary Evans, 58-59: Barcroft Media via Getty Images, 60-61: cl Sergej Razvodovskij, tcl Museumsfoto, Creative Commons Attribution 3.0 Germany license, bl public domain, bcl leemage, tcr DAVID PARKER/SCIENCE PHOTO LIBRARY, c PASCAL GOETGHELUCK/SCIENCE PHOTO LIBRARY, tr © BRENDAN MCDERMID/Reuters/Corbis, bc Sukharevskyy Dmytro, bcr NASA, br Pebble Technology, Creative Commons Attribution-Share Alike 1.0 Generic license, 62-63: l © LASZLO BELICZAY/epa/Corbis, tl © MoodIndigo/Alamy, cb © Heritage Image Partnership Ltd/Alamy, cr © Stéphane Cardinale/People Avenue/Corbis, 64-65: bl National Museum of Education, Ohio, c © ALAN EDWARDS/Alamy, cr Kichigin/Shutterstock, 66-67: cl © Bettmann/Corbis, tcr Getty Images, tl SSPL via Getty Images, bc Bob Orsillo, bcl Redrum0486, Creative Commons Attribution-Share Alike 3.0 Unported license, tcl © Bettmann/Corbis r © STEVE MARCUS/Reuters/Corbis, br bloomua, 68-69: cl jianqing diao, c AFP/Getty Images, cr mrkob, 70-71: tcl Jim Killock, Creative Commons Attribution-Share Alike 2.0 Generic license, c © oliver leedham/Alamy, bl public domain, bc ComputerGeek, Creative Commons Attribution-Share Alike 3.0 Unported license, bcl SRI International, cl AFP/Getty Images, r SHEILA TERRY/SCIENCE PHOTO LIBRARY, bcr SSPL via Getty Images, bc Getty Images, br Raspberry Pi, 72-73: c Getty Images, bcl © AlamyCelebrity/Alamy, GTS Production, br Barcroft Media via Getty Images, bcr Barcroft Media via Getty Images, 74-75: b © Michael Fiscus/Demotix/Corbis, cr © MARK BLINCH/Reuters/Corbis, tr © Zsolt Szigetvary/epa/Corbis, 76-77: c Airbus, tl Sandra Espinet, tr © Piero Cruciatti/Alamy, 78-79: bl Ed Simkins , br Denis Finnin, 0-81: br SSPL via Getty Images

CONTENTS

SO YOU WANT TO INVENT?

Look around you, and you can see inventions everywhere. Inventing happens when somebody sees a problem—and invents something to fix it!

What do you think an inventor looks like? Do you think of a whacky-looking man with mad hair and thick glasses? Think again. Inventors are ordinary people just like you.

You have probably invented things already. Have you ever built anything or created your own games? That's inventing.

Have you ever changed something to make it work better? Maybe part of your bike? That's inventing.

Have you ever puzzled over a problem and thought of a way to solve it? That's inventing.

These toy cars have been made out of beverage cans.

Working out how to fix your bicycle might lead to new ideas.

An old bottle might provide the perfect solution to a problem.

Have you ever used something old and broken to make something new? That's inventing, too.

Have you ever thought of a new way to use an object? That's also inventing.

These low-carbon charcoal fuel disks were invented by Kenyan teenagers. They are made from recycled waste.

This book is full of inventors who have created whole new objects, improved existing ones, or found new and innovative ways to use old objects and used materials. Can you do the same?

THE INVENTION PROCESS

To be an inventor, you need to follow a process, which is made up of a series of steps. This will take your invention from an idea in your head to an actual product.

» STEP 1
IDENTIFY A PROBLEM OR NEED

» STEP 2
BRAINSTORM IDEAS

Make drawings and notes

» STEP 3
WORK UP A DESIGN BRIEF

Does it work?

» STEP 4
MAKE A PROTOTYPE

» STEP 5
TEST THE ITEM

Could you make it better?

» STEP 6
EVALUATE YOUR DESIGN

» STEP 7

MAKE ANY MODIFICATIONS OR CHANGES

» STEP 8

GO INTO PRODUCTION

Protect it from copycats

» STEP 9

PATENT YOUR INVENTION

» STEP 10

DEVELOP BRANDING

» STEP 11

PACKAGE YOUR PRODUCT

Tell other people

» STEP 12

MARKET YOUR INVENTION

Make your product stand out!

RUBIK'S CUBE

Ernö Rubik invented the Rubik's Cube in 1974 when he was teaching art and design in Budapest, Hungary. He liked to invent puzzles to help his students think about three-dimensional (3D) shapes. He created a wooden model of his puzzle, and everyone was fascinated by the way it moved.

Ernö Rubik
1944–present

The cube is made up of 26 movable blocks. Each side has nine squares, and there are 54 colored block faces in total.

1974
First wooden model of the Rubik's Cube is created.

1975
The cube is mass produced.

BÜVÖS
KOCKA

1977
The cube appears in stores in Budapest, Hungary. It is initially called the Magic Cube.

1980
Rubik's Cube is made Toy of the Year.

To start with each side of the cube has one color. Twisting the cube mixes up the colors. There are more than 43 quintillion possible moves, but only one correct solution!

In 1975, a Hungarian toy manufacturer started producing the cubes, and they appeared in the shops in 1977. In 1979, the Rubik's Cube became available around the world. Since then, more than 350 million cubes have been sold.

Rubik's Twist

Rubik's Revenge

» OTHER GAMES

After the success of the original cube, other puzzles were released, including a cube with more pieces called Rubik's Revenge, Rubik's 360 puzzle, Rubik's Twist, and Rubik's TouchCube, a touch-sensitive version with no moving parts.

Rubik's 360

Rubik's TouchCube

1981

1999

2014

You Can Do The Cube, a book telling people how to solve the puzzle, is released and sells 1.5 million copies.

Rubik's Cube celebrates its 25th anniversary.

Beyond Rubik's Cube exhibition opens.

Ernö Rubik

IDENTIFYING A PROBLEM

Inventions are created to solve problems or needs. Identifying a need is the first step in the invention process.

Ernö Rubik was a sculptor and architect teaching at a university in Budapest, Hungary. He needed to teach his students how to tackle three-dimensional (3D) problems and wanted to use something that was fun and educational. To do this, he began designing puzzles for them to solve.

10

Today, architects use computers to make 3D images of their buildings that they can rotate. Rubik did not have access to modern computers. He made models to help his students think about space and the geometry of three dimensions.

In 1974, when he was 29, Rubik created a cube-shape puzzle for his students—the first Rubik's Cube. Each side of the cube was made of colored squares, which the player could move to solve the puzzle.

Robots can be programmed to solve a Rubik's Cube by following a set of mathematical rules.

In order to solve the cube (and make sure that each side only had one color), the students had to be aware of how moves affected all sides of the 3D puzzle.

⛹ STRANGE INVENTIONS

Inventions are often created to solve problems. New objects are being invented every day—some useful and others just plain weird. The ones that don't become popular often fail to solve a problem—or there is already a better solution.

INVENTION:
Dogbrella

Have you ever walked a dog in the rain? They get really wet. Enter the Dogbrella. It's basically an upside-down umbrella that shelters your dog. Most people, however, just rub their dog with a towel afterwards.

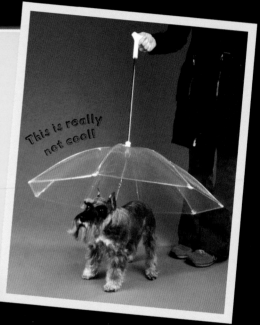

This is really not cool!

INVENTION:
Pizza Scissors

Cutting pizza can be difficult, with all the stringy cheese. There are pizza wheels, but they can run away with you and be dangerous. So how about a pair of pizza scissors? Or you could just use an old-fashioned knife.

INVENTION:
Atomic Car

In 1958, the Ford Nucleon was invented. It was to be a nuclear-powered car, running for about 5,000 miles (8,000 kilometers) without refueling. However, a car carrying a nuclear reactor could cause a huge explosion if it was involved in a crash. The cars were never made.

INVENTION:
Smell-O-Vision

Smell-O-Vision piped scents into the movie theater to make a film more realistic. Thirty different smells, including tobacco and garlic, were pumped into the theaters through tubes beneath the seats. It was used only once, in 1960, and audiences did not like the smells, or the hissing coming from under their seats.

YOUNG INVENTOR'S PORTFOLIO

George Nissen was an enthusiastic gymnast. He had seen circus acts where trapeze artists used their safety nets to bounce and perform tricks. He wanted to create something to help him train, and to do several tricks in a row.

NAME: George Nissen

AGE: 16

INVENTION: The trampoline

YEAR: 1934

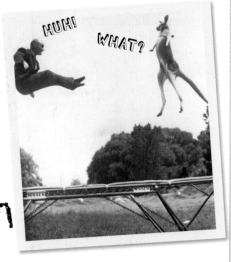

HUH!

WHAT?

More than 25 years after developing the trampoline, George showed off his invention with the help of Victoria, a kangaroo.

BOING!

In 1934, George and his coach built the first prototype, out of an iron frame, a piece of canvas, and some rubber springs. He carried on refining his invention to improve it.

George called his invention the trampoline after the Spanish word *trampolin*, which means "diving board."

In 1956, George set up a factory in Essex, U.K., and made trampolines there for many years. In 2000, trampolining was included as an event in the Olympic Games. Not bad for an invention created by a 16 year old.

» SPACEBALL

George Nissen also invented a game called Spaceball. Two players on each team try to score points by throwing a ball through a hoop—while they are bouncing on trampolines.

BOING!

TELEVISION

Television wasn't invented by one person, but British scientist John Logie Baird was the first to give a public demonstration of television to the world.

Baird used spinning disks to create television pictures. He scanned images with a spinning disk full of tiny holes. Light came through the holes in flashes.

John Logie Baird
1888–1946

Baird used junk to create the first television apparatus—boxes, sewing needles, cardboard, the motor from a fan, and a cookie tin. That makes his invention even more amazing.

1884   1924   1926

Paul Nipkow
1860–1940

1884 — German scientist Paul Nipkow sends images over wires using his invention, the "electric telescope."

1924 — John Logie Baird builds a television and transmits some flickering images across a room.

1926 — Baird demonstrates his television at the Royal Institution in London, U.K.

Baird converted the flashes into electrical signals. He sent the signals and these made a fuzzy picture—the world's first television transmission.

Baird demonstrates an early television set in 1929

Baird's first TV picture

He demonstrated his television to scientists at the Royal Institution in London, U.K. In 1927, he sent pictures from London to Glasgow, and in 1928 he sent the first pictures from Britain to North America.

1928 1940 1946 1962

Baird sends TV pictures from Britain to North America.

Peter Goldmark develops the first commercial color television. It produces colored pictures with the use of a spinning three-colored disk.

RCA Model 630-TS becomes the first mass-produced TV set.

First satellite TV signal relayed from Europe to North America.

BLEEP BLEEP

BRAINSTORM

Brainstorming is a thinking session with the focus on producing ideas. Inventors use brainstorming to come up with new ideas or develop existing ones at the beginning of a project. It can also help inventors come up with answers to difficult problems.

Be very clear about the problem you want to solve before you start. This will help you focus.

When you are brainstorming, write down any thoughts and ideas you have about your project, even if they are completely random. Include ideas about the shape and size of your invention, and how it will work.

Include *everything*. However silly or obvious an idea may seem, make sure you include it. It might spark new ideas later in the process.

Share ideas with others. It's a good idea to bounce thoughts around. Allow people to add their own thoughts to ideas that have already been written down.

Brainstorming is about getting everything out into the open in a safe space, without anything being criticized or praised. Make sure that everyone in the group gets a chance to contribute.

After the brainstorming, have another group discussion to develop and build on the ideas. It helps to have someone act as a facilitator— their job is to make sure everyone is heard and all the ideas are recorded.

YOUNG INVENTOR'S PORTFOLIO

Have you heard of Braille? It is a system to help blind people to read, using a pattern of raised dots that they can feel with their fingertips.

NAME: Louis Braille

AGE: 15

INVENTION: Braille

YEAR: 1824

Can you tell what word this person is reading?

Louis Braille was blinded in an accident when he was 3 years old. He went to a special school for blind people, but found it frustrating that he could not read books and discover things easily for himself.

The alphabet chart for English language Braille

Louis Braille
1809–1852

A	B	C	D	E	F	G	H	I

When he was only 15, Louis created the Braille system that is still used today. He was inspired by "night writing," a system invented by Charles Barbier for the French Army to communicate in the dark. Braille used an awl—a small, pointed tool used for piercing holes in leather—to make raised dots that could be read by touch. In 1829, he published a book about his system.

BRAILLE
By
L. Braille

» BRAILLE WRITER

Today, computers and other devices can be read using Braille, and there are computer printers that **emboss** Braille. It can also be typed using a special typewriter that uses combinations of keys to produce letters, instead of a single key for each letter. The Braille letters are then punched into a piece of paper.

Braille typewriter

J   K   L   M   N   O   P   Q   R   S   T   U   V   W   X   Y   Z

BICYCLE

Bicycles were introduced in the 1800s, and there are now more than a billion of them around the world. The first bicycle was known as a "dandy horse"—it was an odd contraption that the rider had to push along with his or her feet.

The penny-farthing was named after two British coins—the large penny and the small farthing.

By the 1860s, bone-shaking machines, such as the penny-farthing, were rattling about the streets. They made for an uncomfortable ride.

1817

1860s

1885

The dandy horse is invented.

A French inventor, probably Ernest Michaux, adds the first pedals to a bicycle.

Invention of the safety bicycle.

John Kemp Starley
1854 –1901

In 1885, John Kemp Starley invented the "safety bicycle." It had two similar-size wheels, driven by a chain, and a hollow steel frame, which made the bicycle lighter. Crucially, it also had a steerable front wheel—which earlier bicycles did not have.

The "safety bicycle"

Modern racing bikes have light frames made of carbon fiber.

John Dunlop
1840–1921

Bicycle rides became even more comfortable in 1888, when John Dunlop introduced the pneumatic tire, which was cushioned with air.

1888
Pneumatic tires are invented.

1960s
Light racing bicycles with dropped handlebars become popular.

1996
Mountain biking is introduced as an Olympic sport.

DESIGN BRIEF

Once you have worked out what your invention needs to do, it's time to get a design down on paper. It needs to grab people's attention, so appearance can be important, but it still needs to work correctly. To do this, you'll need to create a design **brief**. This is a written document that tells other people how you want your invention to look and function.

Identify the aim of your invention. Make sure you know exactly what the invention needs to do for the finished design to be successful.

Create a design brief. This helps you to organize your ideas in one place. So try to make sure that all the issues you might face when you are making your invention prototype have been thought about.

Make sure you choose the right materials for the job—what qualities do they have that might make them a good choice?

Who is your target audience and who will use your invention? Do they have particular needs that should be considered?

Think about how you want your invention to look. Make rough sketches with notes; they don't have to be perfect.

Keep returning to your brief and use it for reference to guide your work.

Discussing the brief with other people will help to focus your invention's requirements.

These drawings made by Alexander Graham Bell show his thought processes behind inventing the telephone.

» MAKE NOTES

Keep records of your designs. Daniel Drawhaugh wished he had. He claimed to have invented the telephone before Alexander Graham Bell. However, he had no record of his design, so the Supreme Court rejected his claim. Bell had excellent records and was awarded the **patent**—and his place in history.

YOUNG INVENTOR'S PORTFOLIO

Param Jaggi's invention could help save the environment. The young American invented a clever device that turns the carbon dioxide produced by cars into oxygen.

O_2

Algae

NAME: Param Jaggi

AGE: 17

INVENTION:
Car exhaust filter

YEAR: 2011

Param first noticed a problem when he started learning to drive. Cars release a lot of harmful gases into the air, and this damages the environment. He decided to solve this issue by removing the nasty gases.

His invention uses **algae** as a filter. The device plugs into the exhaust pipe of a car, and the algae inside change the gases coming out of the car into clean oxygen. Each device costs around $30.

O_2

PARAM 1

Yuck!

Vrooooom!

Yuck!

Param's algae-packed invention

Param's system, which has now been patented, won an Environmental Protection Agency sustainability award in 2011. In the same year Param won a scholarship to college. He is now working on refining his invention.

O_2

O_2

OTHER USES

Param's invention might be used for more than car emissions—it could possibly be used in power stations to stop pollution from entering the air and even improve the environment.

O_2

MAKING A PROTOTYPE

A **prototype** is the first actual version of an invention. Creating a prototype helps inventors see if their ideas actually work, and it enables them to make changes before going into production. The prototype of the Rubik's Cube was made from wood!

The wooden prototype of the Rubik's Cube

First, create a nonworking model of your design. This is a quick way of seeing how your invention will look.

Designing and making a real working prototype can be expensive, so you may want to test your idea first with a nonworking model before you go on to make a prototype that actually works.

The latest 3D printing technology can create a full working prototype. Inventors can use this to improve their design and avoid costly mistakes.

WHIRR

CLICK!

>Print

3D printers can create a cheap working prototype.

A working model can be used to identify any problems that an invention may have. It might also help to identify any design improvements.

The prototype can be used to help work out the cost of making your invention. Although producing a real prototype can be expensive, mass production brings down the price per unit.

You can also use your prototype to show a function or basic assembled... inventor has a prototype of their invention, it makes it easier for other people to see what it may do.

» KEEP TRYING

In 1978, inventor James Dyson came up with the idea of producing a vacuum cleaner that didn't need a bag. It took him five years to develop, and he created 5,127 prototypes before he produced the first successful model.

This was the first model of the Dyson bagless vacuum cleaner to go on sale.

YOUNG INVENTOR'S PORTFOLIO

In 1905, 11 year old Frank Epperson accidentally invented one of the most popular summer treats. One cold night, he left a drink outside, with a stirring stick still in it. The next morning, Frank discovered that his drink had frozen with the stick inside— and made an ice pop.

NAME: Frank Epperson

AGE: 11

INVENTION: Popsicle®

YEAR: 1905

Frank and his granddaughter enjoy a Popsicle in this photo taken in 1973 to celebrate the 50th anniversary of applying for the patent.

Yippee!

Yummy!

In 1923, 18 years after he first invented the frozen treat, Frank applied for a patent for it. His invention was initially sold as the "Epsicle Ice Pop," but later became the "Popsicle."

The Popsicle Company still exists today and sells more than two billion ice pops a year. The most popular Popsicle flavor is cherry.

EVERYBODY LIKES
Popsicle

THE FROZEN DRINK ON A STICK

Advertisements, such as this poster from the 1950s, helped to make Popsicles even more popular.

» GIANT ICE POP

In 2005, the Snapple company attempted to make the world's largest ice pop. The previous record had been set by a 21-foot (6.4-meter) monster in Holland in 1997. Snapple tried to make a 24-foot (7.6-meter) ice pop in New York—but it melted too fast and firefighters had to hose away the kiwi-strawberry sludge.

XBOX KINECT®

Released in 2010 by Microsoft, the Xbox Kinect uses facial, voice, and gesture recognition to make players feel like they are part of a video game. People have also started using Kinect in more important ways, such as saving lives.

Sensors can recognize faces and voices.

The Kinect uses 3D cameras, laser sensors, and microphones to detect your movements. It then makes the character move the same way.

Moving around controls on-screen characters.

1972

Atari launches Pong, the first commercially successful video game.

1977

Atari releases the Atari 2600, one of the most successful video game consoles ever.

1978

Space Invaders is released.

1988

Sega releases the Mega Drive video game console.

The Kinect can be hooked up to an MRI scanner, then controlled by hand and voice commands. This allows doctors to see pictures to guide their work without touching a keyboard and risking contamination.

It can also be used for keyhole surgery, where it controls the movement of robotic instruments inside the body.

Surgeons using Kinect to perform an operation.

One day, surgeons may be able to use Kinect technology to perform surgery remotely, operating on people in hard-to-reach places, such as disaster zones and battlefields.

1994

Sony releases the PlayStation

2001

Microsoft releases the original Xbox.

2010

Kinect is released

2013

Microsoft releases the Xbox One with

» STEP 5
TESTING

Testing whether an invention works is vital—if it does not function properly, or is not safe, then it's back to the drawing board. It is important to check that a product is easy and safe to use before it goes into mass production.

When you test your prototype, think about how it will work in real life in a variety of different situations. Sometimes, products in development are shown to groups of people as market research to see what they think.

Use the results of your test to refine and change your invention before it goes into production. This saves time and money later on, and it helps to make an invention more successful.

When testing cars, engineers use special dummies that copy how people move in a crash.

Use a "field test" to test your invention in the place and situation where it will be used. While a field test cannot hope to find all of the strengths and weaknesses of a design, it can help you think creatively to improve your work.

Thomas Edison
1847–1931

» LIGHTBULB

When trying to invent the lightbulb, Thomas Edison tested more than 1,600 materials before he found the one that worked. These materials included fishing line, coconut fibers, and the hair from a colleague's beard. His notes on the testing filled more than 40,000 pages. In 1879, he found that carbonized bamboo kept the bulb lit for more than 40 hours.

These toys are being tested inside a laboratory to make sure they are safe.

Testing an invention for safety is crucial. If an invention is not safe to use, it cannot be sold. Testing helps make any safety problems obvious and can stop something that is not safe from going onto the market.

YOUNG INVENTOR'S PORTFOLIO

Emily Cummins started inventing things when she was four years old. She used to make toys out of scraps with her granddad in his garden shed. Today, she still makes things—but these inventions could change the world.

NAME: Emily Cummins

AGE: 18

INVENTION: Evaporative refrigerator

YEAR: 2005

Emily holding her evaporative refrigerator in her grandfather's shed, where she has created most of her inventions.

In 2006, Emily entered one of her inventions into a sustainable design competition—a pullable water carrier for use in developing countries. Her device won her a Technology Woman of the Future award.

She has also invented a type of refrigerator powered by dirty water and **evaporation**. The refrigerator runs without electricity and it can be built using barrels, car parts, and easy-to-find materials. It can be used to keep medicines and food cool.

Solar panels provide electricity in sunny, remote areas, such as this hut in the Sahara.

» REMOTE POWER

Getting electricity to homes requires a lot of equipment— including generators, pylons, and cables. Some countries can't afford to build the equipment needed to get electricity everywhere, so remote places need to come up with their own, local sources.

This radio is powered by clockwork. Turning the handle charges up a battery.

Emily worked on her plan during a gap year in Namibia, Africa, and gave out the plans for it in townships across southern Africa so people could build their own.

MP3 MUSIC PLAYER

An MP3 media player is a digital audio player that stores and plays MP3 files and other media. MP3 files take up less storage memory than previous files, so you can fit more onto a music player. MP3 players, such as iPods, can store thousands of tunes on one tiny machine.

Karlheinz Brandenburg
1954–present

Inventor Thomas Edison's phonograph recorded sounds on a metal cylinder.

Karlheinz Brandenburg is a German scientist and mathematician who began developing the files that would become MP3s in 1977. He had already developed two earlier versions—the MP1 and the MP2. In 1996, he created the greatly improved MP3 and patented the idea.

1877

Thomas Edison invents the phonograph to create sound recordings.

1889

Emile Berliner starts selling flat disks and players called gramophones.

1982

Compact discs (CDs) are launched.

Brandenburg also developed an MP3 player, but it was not very reliable. In 1997, Tomislav Uzelac of Advanced Media Products created the AMP MP3 Playback Engine, one of the first reliable MP3 players.

Apple's iPod is the world's most popular MP3 player.

Portable MP3 players began to appear in 1999, but they were really heavy and bulky. Apple introduced iPod MP3 players in 2001, eight months after they released the software iTunes. People use iTunes to buy MP3 versions of music and load the files directly onto their iPod.

1996
MP3s is patented.

2001
Apple iPod is introduced

2003
iTunes Music Store is launched.

2012
350 millionth iPod is sold

EVALUATION

Evaluation is an important part of any project—especially creating a new invention! It is important to think carefully about how the invention works, and whether it needs changes. Evaluation can identify and look at any problems that have arisen during the testing process.

Does the invention actually work? Can it be used in the way that was intended when it was designed? If not, changes may need to be made.

This car is being tested to make sure that it performs well and is safe.

Is the invention made as simply as possible—or has it been overcomplicated? Are there things that can be left out or modified?

Is the invention safe as it is or are changes needed?

Is the idea really new? Are there other very similar products available? Even if there are, the new invention may be a better solution to the problem.

Will the invention cost too much to produce or make in bulk?

Will the invention work well and last, or will it break?

Will people want to use the invention? If so, why?

» WARNING!

Proper evaluation of a product is essential—skip this stage and it could fail spectacularly. The Segway, for example—a kind of motorized step or scooter—worked well and had a lot of publicity, but it failed to sell well and lost a lot of money. Its inventors hadn't properly evaluated the product's function and usefulness in everyday life.

The Segway worked well but problems over where to ride, park, and charge it led to its failure.

YOUNG INVENTOR'S PORTFOLIO

While working in a factory, a girl called Margaret Knight saw a horrible accident. A steel-tipped shuttle flew out of a weaving loom, hitting and injuring one of her friends.

NAME: Margaret Knight

AGE: 12

INVENTION: Shuttle restraining device

YEAR: 1850

In the 1800s, children often worked in factories to help their families earn a living. Accidents were common and many children were hurt.

RUUUNNN!

Woooosh!

In 1850, Margaret invented a solution to the problem. She created a device to restrain the shuttle so it could not fly out of place as it zoomed back and forth along the weaving loom.

» MORE IDEAS

Margaret was a clever girl, and she went on to invent other things. In 1871, she invented the machine that makes the square-bottom paper bags that are used to carry groceries. When she applied for her patent, she had to fight the claim of a man called Charles Annan. He said that the design was his and claimed that a woman could not have invented such a machine.

M.E. KNIGHT

M. E. KNIGHT.
Paper-Bag Machine.
No. 9,202.
Reissued May 18, 1880.
Fig. 1.
Fig. 2.
Witnesses.
Inventor

This is the patent form for Margaret's paper bag machine.

DIGITAL CAMERA

Cameras have been around in different forms since the first successful photograph was taken around 1826–27 by French inventor Nicéphore Niépce. By 1900, photography had become very popular. The recent invention of digital cameras allows us to take and share photos in an instant.

Steve Sasson
1950–present

Memory card

Unlike old cameras, digital cameras do not need film. They save images electronically on memory cards.

The first digital camera was built in 1975 by the engineer Steve Sasson, who worked for U.S. manufacturer Kodak. It weighed 8 pounds (3.6 kg) and recorded black-and-white images onto a cassette tape. It was not put on sale because the images were of very low resolution.

1826-27   1883-29   1900

First successful photograph is taken by Niépce, of the view from his window.

George Eastman develops photographic film to replace large plates.

Box Brownie camera is released.

In 1989, the first digital camera went on sale in Japan. It used an internal memory card to store images. The following year, digital cameras went on sale in the United States—but they cost nearly $1000.

Today, inexpensive digital cameras are available and most cell phones now have them, too.

1948

Polaroid release the first instant camera.

1975

First digital camera is built.

2000

First cell phone with a camera is released.

2013

Nokia releases a phone with a 41-megapixel camera.

MODIFICATION

The original Cube (above) was modified (below) to meet western safety standards.

When you "modify" something, you change it. Making a **modification** to an invention means changing it to make it better or more effective. Sometimes inventions are modified after they have been tested; others are modified after they are on the market, when somebody thinks of an improvement.

A technician testing a toy robot.

Hmmmm?

Inventors consider a range of questions after they have tested and evaluated their invention. Could it be improved by using a different material?

Could the invention be adapted so it fits its purpose better?

Is the shape right? Does it need to be more streamlined so it can move quicker, or do the edges need to be rounded for safety reasons?

Could the invention be used in different ways, or for different purposes? Sometimes this is only discovered after testing when the inventor is thinking about his or her findings.

Would the invention work better if it was made to a different scale, either smaller or bigger than the prototype?

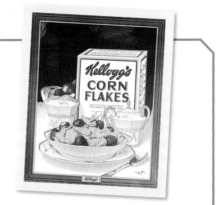

» CORNFLAKES

Cornflakes were invented by accident while Keith Kellogg and his brother were researching healthy hospital meals. Having left some bread dough to sit for hours, Keith discovered the wheat in it had turned flaky. He toasted the flakes, and found the patients loved them. He then modified his invention, using corn instead of wheat. He launched his company in 1906—and this later became known as Kellogg's.

Are similar inventions available? If market research shows there are, inventors should be prepared to make changes to be sure they offer an improved version—it doesn't mean an invention has failed.

Have you ever cycled when it is dark? It is important that you can be easily seen to avoid having an accident. That is why cyclists wear clothing with reflective strips and have lights on their bicycles.

NAME: Adam Kassell

AGE: 14

INVENTION: Super-bright LED bicycle clips

YEAR: 2012

Fourteen year old Adam Kassell, from Worthing in West Sussex in the U.K., went one step farther to be sure of cycling safety. In 2012, he designed super-bright **LED** bicycle clips that are clipped around the ankles and can be programmed to spell out words. These lights make cyclists more visible to car drivers, making cycling in the dark much safer.

Bike lights and reflective strips on clothing are essential equipment for cyclists.

In 2012, Adam was one of two winners of the "We Made It!" competition, which was set up to encourage young inventors in the UK. Prototypes of the winning ideas are created and tested. The aim of the annual competition is to encourage teenagers to think about careers in manufacturing.

Adam and the design for his bicycle clips (below) beat off more than 350 entries to win the competition.

PRODUCTION

Production means making copies of something so that they are ready to sell. The prototype of the Rubik's Cube was made by hand, but the real cubes are made in factories. These steps explain the different parts of production for a Rubik's Cube—the process differs for other products.

A car production assembly line.

Plastic pellets

A Rubik's Cube is made from plastic pellets. These are melted and the molten plastic is injected into a mold.

Two parts of the mold are brought together to create a cavity in the shape of a part of the Rubik's Cube. It could be an edge, a corner, or a center piece.

The plastic cools in the mold, and it turns hard. When the mold is opened, the cube pieces are removed and the process starts again.

Cube pieces

The completed parts are dropped in containers and inspected to make sure they are not faulty or damaged.

All steps in any production process involve checks to see if everything is going well.

» INSPECTION

Checking a Rubik's Cube involves a lot more than just looking at each piece. The thickness, length, and width of each piece are checked with a caliper, a micrometer, and even a microscope.

A caliper gives accurate measurements.

The pieces are taken to the assembly line, where they are put together to make a cube. The center parts are attached to the nylon core.

Colored labels are added to the cube. These are laminated with a special covering to protect them and stop them from peeling off.

YOUNG INVENTOR'S PORTFOLIO

Catherine Wong invented a health test that could save the lives of millions of people, and all while she was still at school. This 16 year old invented a tiny device that can be connected to a cell phone to show a person's heartbeat on its screen.

NAME: Catherine Wong

AGE: 16

INVENTION:
Cellular electrocardiogram (cell phone heart test)

YEAR: 2012

THUMP!

THUMP!

This patient is attached to an ECG machine.

Catherine's device works like a portable electrocardiogram. Also called an ECG or EKG, these often large pieces of equipment are used at a hospital or doctor's office to measure how the patient's heart is beating.

Wong's clever device can be used in remote places, where people do not have access to hospitals with sophisticated health-care machinery.

The device is attached to the patient's skin with a sticky patch and sends signals wirelessly, using bluetooth, to the phone. The phone converts the signals into an image that a doctor can read. The image can then be e-mailed to a doctor anywhere in the world. This could be vital for identifying whether a patient has had a heart attack and needs to go to a hospital quickly for life-saving treatment.

CHOCOLATE BAR

Chocolate is made from roasted cocoa beans. In the Aztec and Mayan cultures of North and Central America, a chocolate drink was used in religious ceremonies. In Europe, chocolate was sweetened by adding sugar and milk. It was first made into bars in the nineteenth century.

The Mayans drank chocolate with added corn or chile.

Founded in 1761, Joseph Fry and Sons started out making chocolate tablets for drinking chocolate. In 1847, the company created the first chocolate bar.

1502

Chocolate is brought to Europe from the Americas by Christopher Columbus.

Christopher Columbus 1451–1506

1650

Chocolate becomes a popular drink in Europe.

1847

Joseph Fry and Son create the first chocolate bar.

Fry's chocolate bars were made in factories.

The firm first produced Fry's Chocolate Cream Bar in 1866, and it is still in production today. They went on to make more than 220 products in the next decade, including the first chocolate Easter egg in 1873.

Keen to try new things, Joseph Fry's grandson discovered how to mix cocoa powder, extracted cocoa butter, and sugar to create solid chocolate that was smoother than the chocolate tablets. The result could be molded into bars and eaten.

Fry poured chocolate over fruit-flavor creamy centers.

FRY'S CHOCOLATE CREAM

J.S. FRY & SONS. Ltd. MAKERS OF PURE CONCENTRATED

1875
Swiss chocolatier Daniel Peter creates the first milk chocolate bar.

1919
The chocolate companies Cadbury and Fry and Sons merge.

FAIRTRADE

2009
Cadbury's Dairy Milk becomes Fairtrade, raising the living standards of cocoa farmers in Ghana.

» STEP 9
PATENTS

Did you know that ideas and inventions can be stolen? But they can also be protected. Governments around the world issue patents to stop people from copying ideas. A patent gives inventors control over the way their inventions are made, used, or sold.

A new idea—such as an invention—is called "**intellectual property**," and it can be protected by applying for a patent.

A patent is a document that says that the registered inventor has the right to stop other people from copying their idea. Nobody else can make, sell, or use another person's patented invention without permission.

This is the 1983 U.S. patent for the Rubik's Cube. The cube was first patented in Hungary and trademarked as "The Magic Cube." This changed to the "Rubik's Cube" for international markets.

U.S. Patent

Mar. 29, 1

Fig.1

Fig.5

Fig.1

Fig.6

Fig.11

Fig.12

» YOUNG INVENTORS

Did you know there are no age restrictions on applying for a patent? The youngest person to be awarded a patent was a four year old girl from Texas, who invented an aid for grasping round knobs on drawers and doors.

Patents have been awarded to some strange inventions, such as a helmet-mounted gun and an umbrella hat.

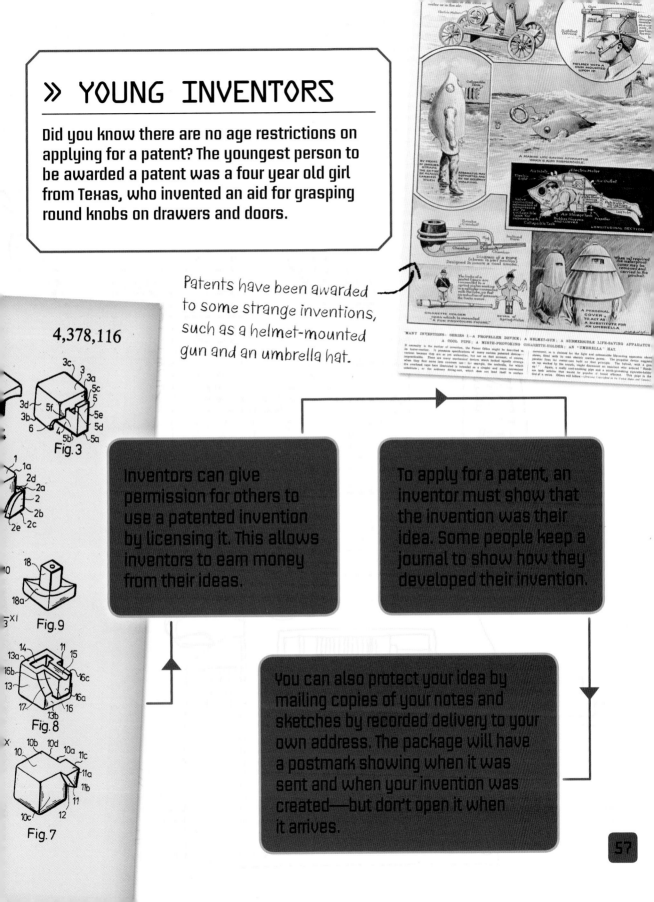

4,378,116

Fig. 3

Fig. 9

Fig. 8

Fig. 7

Inventors can give permission for others to use a patented invention by licensing it. This allows inventors to earn money from their ideas.

To apply for a patent, an inventor must show that the invention was their idea. Some people keep a journal to show how they developed their invention.

You can also protect your idea by mailing copies of your notes and sketches by recorded delivery to your own address. The package will have a postmark showing when it was sent and when your invention was created—but don't open it when it arrives.

Milan's solar panel can power a light or charge a cell phone using hair.

NAME: Milan Karki

AGE: 18

INVENTION:
Human hair solar panel

YEAR: 2009

Imagine growing up in a world without electricity. No lights at the touch of a switch, no computers, and no TV. Milan Karki grew up in a remote area of Nepal in a small village that was not connected to the electricity grid.

Many parts of rural Nepal are without electricity, and even those areas connected to the grid have nearly daily power cuts.

Milan studied hard and became a science student in Kathmandu. His education paid off—when he was 18, he invented a cheap solar energy panel—made using human hair instead of silicon.

The solar panel prototype costs $40 to produce—up to four times cheaper than existing solar panels that have a similar capacity of 9 volts—and would be cheaper still if it was mass produced. It makes an already "green" energy source even more environmentally friendly, because hair is a renewable resource.

WRISTWATCH

Watches have been around since the seventeenth century—but early watches were very different from the wristwatches of today. Carried in the pocket, these watches had mechanical mechanisms powered by springs.

A watch worn in World War I

The first watches were pocket watches, which were held on a chain. In the 1900s, the first wristwatches appeared, but they were worn only by women.

This changed with the outbreak of World War I, when soldiers needed quick access to the time, and their hands free for weapons.

1600s	1812	1904	1914
Pocket watches are invented.	Abraham-Louis Breguet creates a watch to fit on the wrist of the Queen of Naples.	Aviator Alberto Santos Dumont (right) has a wristwatch made for him to wear while flying.	Wristwatches for men appear during World War I.

Mechanical watch mechanism

Mechanical watches need to be wound up by hand. Today, most watches are electronic and contain a tiny, vibrating quartz crystal.

The latest smartwatches let you make phone calls and surf the Internet.

Electricity makes the crystal vibrate at a constant speed. These vibrations are used to set the time.

Watches now have other functions, including stopwatches, alarms, and calendars. Some modern watches can even connect to the Internet and forecast the weather.

1965

NASA astronauts start wearing Omega wristwatches.

1972

The first digital watch goes on sale.

2013

The Pebble and Samsung Galaxy Gear smartwatches are launched. They can connect to the Internet and cell phones.

BRANDING

Branding includes the style and appearance of packaging, and it also includes the name of a product and the way it is presented. A good name is really important.

Ernö Rubik's name is a key component of the Rubik's Cube brand.

Sometimes products are named using the inventor's name. The Rubik's Cube is named after its inventor, Ernö Rubik. His name has now become famous due to the success of his cube.

Companies often employ advertising agencies to come up with ideas on how to present their products. Advertisements exist to make people want to buy products.

Ferrero Rocher's packaging, advertising, and even its name create a feeling of luxury.

Leaflets and other literature accompanying an item also contribute to branding. The Rubik's Cube came with an instruction manual to help people solve the puzzle—but it was also part of the branding. It used images and text to show that the cube was educational and fun.

Advertisements also help create a brand, and they often emphasize the lifestyle or mood that can be "bought" along with the product. For example, a type of chocolate might be branded in such a way as to suggest an indulgent, luxurious lifestyle.

Rubik's Cube purse

» BRAND RUBIK'S

People have liked the Rubik's brand so much that all kinds of other products have been made. There are Rubik's purses, furniture made using huge blocks of Rubik's Cubes, Rubik's Cube sneakers, Rubik's Cube lamps—and Rubik's Cube cakes!

Rubik's Cube chair

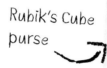

YOUNG INVENTOR'S PORTFOLIO

NAME: Hannah Haas

AGE: 13

INVENTION:
Sensory wallpaper

YEAR: 2008

Hannah's invention was the Grand Prize Winner in the 2008 Bubble Wrap Competition for Young Inventors.

In 2008, 13 year old Hannah Haas invented a sensory wallpaper for special sensory rooms. It can be used to help stimulate children with autism spectrum disorders. Autism is a brain disorder which can make it hard to make sense of the world.

Hannah wrote an essay to describe her invention and entered it into a competition run by the Bubble Wrap® company. She described how children with autism often find stroking their hands across a textured surface calming.

Bubble Wrap has small air bubbles trapped in a plastic sheet.

POP!

CRACKLE!

Sensory rooms, such as this one, are filled with equipment and decorations that are designed to stimulate mental activity.

Sensory wallpaper ensures that autistic children have the means to calm themselves built into their own environment, making their lives more comfortable.

» OTHER INVENTIONS

Other winners of the annual Bubble Wrap competition include wrist supports to help with carpal tunnel syndrome, special curtains to make refrigerators more efficient, a water-saving device for toilets and a cost-effective cosmetic skin covering for artificial limbs to use in developing countries.

TELEPHONE

The electric telegraph was invented in the 1840s, and the age of the telephone began. Alexander Graham Bell worked on the idea of sending voice messages along telegraph wires. His telephone was patented in 1876 and history was made.

Alexander Graham Bell
1847–1922

In 1946, Bell Labs created a system that allowed users to make calls from their cars.

The history of cell phones began during the 1940s, when handheld devices were used by the army to communicate during World War II. It developed further with the use of two-way radios in police cars, taxis, and trains. These early phones were big and bulky, and used a lot of power.

1840s	1876	1940s	1946	1973
Electric telegraph is invented.	Telephone is patented.	Handheld communication devices are used during World War II.	Car phones come onto the market.	First cell phone call is made.

In 1973, Martin Cooper, a manager at Motorola, made the first ever cell phone call. He rang Joel Engel, the head of research at Bell Labs. This first cell phone weighed 2½ pounds (1.1 kg) and was a huge 5 inches (13 cm long) and 1¾ inches (4.45 cm) wide! It allowed just 30 minutes of talk and took ten hours to charge.

Martin Cooper testing the cell phone

Cell phones have come a long way since the early 1970s and are now tiny and reliable. Modern "smartphones" can connect users to the Internet, like a tiny computer. The latest technology also allows for people to enjoy streamed radio and TV programs on their phones.

1991
Invention of technology that leads to the introduction of WiFi.

2001
3G technology is introduced.

2004
Mass-market Voice over Internet Protocol (VoIP) services allow for people to use the Internet to make voice and video calls.

2007
Apple release the iPhone.

2009
4G technology is launched.

PACKAGING

Packaging helps to protect a product, keeping it safe during transit—the journey from the factory to a store, and from the store to the purchaser's house. Packaging also needs to be attractive, so that people notice the product and want to buy it.

Packaging has to protect the product inside. Sometimes a cardboard box is used, because it is sturdy and can cushion the product if it gets dropped or bumped. If cardboard is used, a picture of the product usually features on the outside.

Packaged products will often be stored and transported in crates or on pallets.

This Rubik's Cube packaging includes a protective cardboard case and a window to show people what's inside.

Sometimes clear blister plastic packs are used, because they help protect a product while also showing people what is inside the package.

Packages need to be a shape that can easily be packed on pallets or in crates. They can then be transported to stores cheaply and efficiently.

Packaging contains information about the product. This information tells people how to use the product safely and how to get the most enjoyment from it.

A code reader identifies the cost and important shipping information.

Good packaging should make a product attractive to buyers.

The packaging also contains information about how the product should be handled, where it needs to be sent, and how much it costs. This information is usually contained in a special code that can be read using code readers.

⬛ INVENTION TIMELINE

RASPBERRY PI

When Eben Upton, a physicist and computer engineer, was teaching at Cambridge University, he realized that computers were so expensive that it was difficult for everyone to afford them, which could make learning difficult.

Eben Upton
1978–present

All the Pi's working parts are visible.

He decided to invent a small, cheap computer that could make computing accessible to all. He created the Raspberry Pi.

Everything has been done to keep the cost of the computer low. It does not come with a plastic case or a DVD drive. As a result, each Raspberry Pi costs only about $25.

1820s

Charles Babbage designs a difference engine, a mechanical computer.

Charles Babbage
1791–1871

1936

Konrad Zuse builds the Z1, the first freely programmable computer.

1964

Douglas Engelbart invents the computer mouse.

The Raspberry Pi Foundation was set up as a charity with the aim of making computers affordable for all.

This robot is powered by a Raspberry Pi.

The original model had 256 MB of RAM.

1984

Apple releases the Macintosh computer.

1989

Tim Berners-Lee develops a system that becomes the World Wide Web.

Tim Berners-Lee 1955–present

2006

Eben Upton devises the Raspberry Pi.

2012

The Raspberry Pi is released.

MARKETING

Marketing is the process of making a product look attractive to customers. Products are marketed through advertising on the television or radio, at the movie theater, in newspapers and magazines, online, and as billboards. Advertising is everywhere.

Marketing a product means persuading people to buy it. This is often achieved by suggesting that the product will make a person's life better—more fun, for example. Advertisements of the Rubik's Cube show people having a good time.

Eye-catching displays in stores help market products, because they make people notice them. Advertisers use special stands and settings to make store and window displays.

Special versions of the Rubik's Cube, such as this leather and nickel-trimmed one, create extra publicity.

The world's smallest Rubik's Cube also generates interest.

Images help advertisements to be bright and interesting. Photographers and graphic designers work hard to make advertisements as attractive as possible.

Advertising billboards in London.

Copywriters come up with jingles and slogans to help sell a product. Look for examples around you. Musicians write catchy music and songs to help make the advertisement noticeable, so that people remember it.

» CUBIST ART

The Cube Works Studio from Canada re-create works of art using Rubik's Cubes. The artists twist the cubes to form patterns and the cubes are then put together to replicate famous works of art and completely new pieces, including *The Last Supper* by Leonardo da Vinci (below).

Created in 2009, this artwork was 8½ feet high and 17 feet wide and made up of 4,050 cubes.

COMPETITIONS AND CLUBS

There are a lot of competitions and clubs for young inventors around the world. It's a good way to make you think hard about your ideas and planning, and because you have a deadline, it really focuses the mind. It's also a great way to make friends with other inventors. Many science museums and loads of large companies run competitions— look on the Internet and find one that suits you. Good luck!

You might also like to explore some Web sites for inventors, or join a club. Have a look at these useful sites:

Speed cubers get some practise in at the 2013 Rubik's Cube Championships in Las Vegas.

Maker Faire
http://makerfaire.com

Let's Get Inventin'
http://www.younginventors.tv

Academy of Applied Science
http://www.aas-world.org

Science Museum, London, U.K.
http://www.sciencemuseum.org.uk

Liberty Center, New York
http://lsc.org

A Canadian competitor attempts to solve the puzzle blindfolded.

Arranging competitions is a great way to promote and market your invention. For example, there are competitions where people try to solve the Rubik's Cube as quickly as possible, with some even using their feet or wearing a blindfold.

Too easy to solve the puzzle with your hands? Try doing it with your feet.

These competitions are a great way of gathering people together in one room. You can use these events to get publicity and to gain exposure in newspapers as well as on the radio and television.

SUMMARY

So, invention is a process. From the first idea, there are many stages to go through on the journey to a product that can be used and sold.

Creating and developing your invention is hard work and not something that can be achieved overnight. There are many stages you will have to go through before your idea has been perfected, but there's no better feeling than seeing your creation become a reality.

AIRBUS
concept plane

Think about what you would like to invent, or talk it through with friends, and always keep a record of any ideas you might have—you never know which one might work.

Will you create a world-changing mode of transport, a new way of making things, or an ecological device that can reduce pollution or energy consumption and save the planet?

» LATEST INVENTIONS

3D printers can produce items, such as these shoes, quickly and cheaply.

These artificial trees could draw carbon dioxide from the atmosphere and cut pollution.

The latest designs and materials will produce airplanes that can fly farther and more economically.

F-EIAI

You've read about inventors both young and old who have had an impact on the way we run our lives. Now it's your turn. You might not get it right first time, and it will be hard work, but one thing is certain— inventing is exciting!

"Genius is 1 percent inspiration and 99 percent perspiration."
Thomas Edison

GLOSSARY

ALGAE
A group of living organisms that produce the energy they need to live and survive from sunlight but do not have the structures found in plants, such as leaves and roots.

BRAINSTORMING
A way of thinking creatively, either alone or in a group, to come up with a solution to a problem. Inventors use brainstorming to come up with a range of ideas that can be used to develop an invention.

BRANDING
An image or idea used to sell a product. Branding can include packaging and the colors and images used for advertising, as well as the product's name.

BRIEF
A set of instructions that clearly tells someone how you want an object to look and perform.

DESIGN
A design is a detailed plan for something. It helps inventors work out how a product can be made.

EMBOSS
To push or raise something so that it sits above the surrounding area.

EVALUATION
After an invention has been tested, it needs to be evaluated—that means working out if the product works properly and does the things that it was intended to do when it was designed. It also makes sure that the product is safe to use and will not harm anyone.

EVAPORATION
The process of changing from a liquid into a gas. Water evaporates to form water vapor. Evaporation causes the body of liquid to cool slightly, until it is a similar temperature to its surroundings.

INTELLECTUAL PROPERTY

An idea—such as a plan for an invention—can be intellectual property. It can be stolen like any other property, so it needs to be protected by law. Patents can be registered to protect intellectual property from being copied.

LED

Short for Light-Emitting Diode, these are special lights that emit more light per watt than normal lightbulbs. They are used in all sorts of devices, from traffic signals to bicycle lights.

MARKETING

Marketing means a plan for advertising and selling things. Many businesses have marketing plans to help them predict how well a product will sell, and how many units need to be produced.

MASS PRODUCTION

Making things in large numbers is known as mass production. This is usually done in a factory, using machinery. The production costs are reduced dramatically because the objects are made in large numbers.

MODIFICATION

Modification means changing or adapting things. Inventions are often modified after they have been tested to make improvements.

PATENT

A patent is a legal document that protects an idea or invention. Inventors apply for patents so that other people cannot use, produce, or sell things that were not their own original idea.

PROTOTYPE

A prototype is a working model of an invention. It is created to make sure an idea works, and to iron out any problems before it goes into production. Prototypes are sometimes used during the process of applying for a patent to prove that an invention belongs to a particular inventor.

INDEX